In the group's own w
and pictures

KNIGHT BOOKS
Hodder and Stoughton

Copyright © Deniece Pearson/5 Star 1987. First published by Knight Books 1987. ISBN 0-340-42620-9
Printed in Great Britain for Hodder and Stoughton Paperbacks, a division of Hodder and Stoughton Ltd,
Mill Road, Dunton Green, Sevenoaks, Kent TN13 2YE by John Blackburn Limited, Leeds.
Hodder and Stoughton Editorial Office: 47 Bedford Square, London WC1B 3DP. All rights reserved

We would all like to dedicate this book to YOU and take this opportunity to say a great big thank you from the bottom of our hearts, for playing such an important role in our lives and our careers.
Thank you for all your support and enthusiasm, for all your gifts and letters, but most of all for your loyalty, which has made us what we are today. It's having you out there in our audience that makes our music come alive, and it's meeting you on our tours which gives us the greatest pleasure in this music industry.
This book has been written specially for YOU.

Introduction

IT'S ME and Doris (writes Deniece) who are the real photography fiends in the Pearson family; everywhere we go we take our trusty old cameras (they're nothing *flashy* if you'll excuse the pun!) and everything we do gets 'snapped' for posterity – and now for this special book of memories.

This is my diary of our first travels in Europe and America. But the 5 Star phenomenon really began back in Romford, Essex, on the north-eastern edge of London. Romford was once famous only for its brewery – but now the brewery has us to compete with!

One fateful day in 1983, Doris, Delroy, Stedman, Lorraine and I gathered around the dining table in our old home and made a very important decision about our future. It was a decision that was serious and precious to us then, and one that's become rewarding and successful for us today. We wanted to form a group together, so we made a pact. We said, 'Right, we've got to do our very best, we've got to be strong, to keep straight and we must be a *complete* success!'

And now in 1987, just four years later, not only have we become a success, we've managed to keep the whole sensation going from strength to strength. When I look back I find it incredible to think that in so little time we've managed to achieve as much recognition as some of the music industry's most legendary groups. Just imagine – a B.P.I. award for the Best British Group!

We find our work enjoyable and fulfilling. We love working hard and doing our best because we've always believed that doing things this way pays off in the end.

We began our career in the recording studio and quickly moved to TV studios and started making videos. But the most frightening and nerve-racking experience still lay ahead of us. Can you guess what that was? It was our first concert tour – performing live on stage for the first time in front of thousands of people.

For us, that was the biggest challenge in the world. We each experienced strange feelings about that first tour, because even though we knew it would have to come at some time in our career, none of us could imagine it happening in real life!

September 14th 1986 was the momentous day when the music world opened its arms to the 5 Star Crunchie Tour. (It was sponsored by the chocolate bar manufacturers.) There was such a demand for tickets that we soon felt as if we'd taken the world by storm! We were actually presented with trophies for selling out in record time! But more people wanted to come and see us than there were dates and seats available, and just as we were about to go on the road, our fan club was besieged by requests for more concerts.

The whole situation seemed to be getting out of control and we didn't know what to do. But one person did, and he just happened to be the wisest businessman and most accomplished musician, songwriter, producer and manager we know. None other than our father, Buster Pearson!

This is what Daddy said at the time: 'It was the biggest thing I've ever encountered with such a young

continued overleaf

Introduction
continued from previous page

group in the whole of my twenty-eight years in the music industry! I had to check out all the requests for extra venues and make sure my children realised how much harder work a few extra dates could be.

'They told me to go ahead and book them because even though they knew they had a great task ahead of them, their main aim and desire was to satisfy their fans. If there's one thing 5 Star have the greatest respect for, apart from their parents, it's their fans.'

And yes, that's exactly how we felt, and we're very proud of the fact that even though we're so young, we've managed to achieve such high standards in such a short time.

Many people compare our success with that of the Jackson Five, for obvious reasons. They, too, were a family famous for their dance routines, costumes and vocals, But we feel we've been pretty well organised from the very start - for example, we own our own record label - and it's things like that that keep you one step ahead of the rest.

We're also proud of our album success, because sales have been good not only in Britain, but also in America. Our first album, *Luxury of Life*, reached platinum and stayed in the album charts for one and a half years, until our second album, *Silk And Steel*, beat it to the platinum spot.

But that isn't all. Do you know (and read this piece of information very carefully!) we're now officially the youngest group since the seventies' glam band, the Bay City Rollers, to top the British albums' chart!

Well, all we have to say about this is that we feel, and we hope all our fans feel, that we've discovered a true and winning formula for success. We're determined to keep working hard and can't wait to see what the future holds for us.

We've been given a talent which we will always try to use to the full, and we intend to *keep on* taking the world by storm!

Delroy

Lorraine Stedman Doris

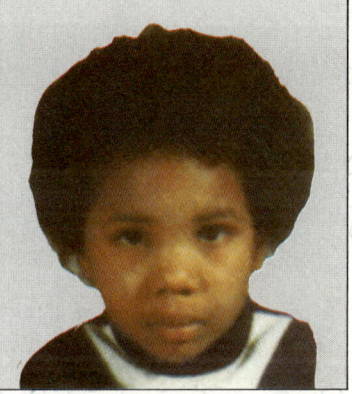
Deniece

In the beginning – The Nappy Brigade!

Even a musical family like ours had to learn to walk and talk before we could sing and dance. We were crawling around on our Romford living-room carpet on all-fours long before we were capable of standing behind a microphone or twirling around on stage!

So before I tell you about our tales and travels as 5 Star, let's start at the *very* beginning with some memories of the Pearson nappy brigade!

Deniece
❛ Mummy tells me that I was a very strong and fearless baby, and I was never afraid of the dark. She says when I was only two years old she used to hear the patter of my tiny feet going down the stairs at midnight! She had to keep an eye on me because sometimes she'd catch me walking around in the dark with Delroy in my arms! ❜

Stedman
❛ I was the lightest in weight and the longest in length as a baby. The funniest thing about me, as Mum recalls, was my head! Now a new-born baby normally has a bit of a wobbly head, but mine wasn't like an ordinary head because my neck was so long.

It was completely out of proportion to the rest of my body, and this meant that every time Mum tried to feed me, my head wouldn't keep still. It kept rocking backwards and forwards while she was trying to get the spoon in my mouth – I had no control over it! Well, all babies have funny characteristics at some stage in their lives, don't they? ❜

Doris
❛ When we were babies Mummy said I was the one who ate the most. I remember one day when I was about two years old she had brought home a chocolate bar for Stedman. Being the little pig that I was, I whipped it out of her bag, unwrapped it and ate it in seconds flat.

I got in such a mess that Mum had to wash and dress me again because we were due to visit our cousins, and as soon as we got there I had a really bad tummy ache and ended up having to swallow a big spoon-ful of cod liver oil. Ugh! ❜

Lorraine
❛ When I was a baby I was incredibly tiny, so tiny that Mummy had to make me special clothes, much smaller than those of the average baby. Would you believe that I was actually small enough to fit into dolls' clothes? ❜

Delroy
❛ As a toddler I was the biggest in the family. I came out of my nappies the quickest, and naturally I walked at the youngest age. I suppose that this was when I first realised exactly how *cool* I was. ❜

TV Times

OUR television début, and the first major breakthrough in our career, was when we had a slot on the *Pebble Mill At One* show in Birmingham back in 1983, which Dad helped make possible for us.
This was our first taste of what television was really like, and I don't know what *you* thought about us if you saw that programme, but this is what was going through *our* minds at the time...

Deniece

❛ I remember walking into the TV studio and noticing all the equipment; there were cables tangled up all over the floor and cameras waiting to capture our performance when we finally went on the air.

I started to think about all the people who'd be watching us and it made me feel nervous at first. But deep down inside I felt proud of myself – for appearing on television is something that most people only dream about, and something you have to work hard for. I felt proud of us all because we *had* worked hard, and there we were!

One thing in particular that surprised me was the size of the TV studio. Watching the programme at home, I'd always had the impression that *Pebble Mill* had a very big set, but in reality, it was smaller than our living-room. Did that mean, I wondered, that we'd look twice life-size on television? The amazing thing is that TV *does* create the illusion of making you look about half a stone heavier, and that may be why people who meet us on the street always say how thin we look. I suppose it's an advantage in a way! ❜

Lorraine

❛ I remember when the floor manager came up to our dressing-room to fetch us we all started fiddling around, fixing our make-up and clothes, because no one wanted to be the first to walk into the studio. Then, when we finally got on the set, they played our music and my mind went completely blank. Good job it was only a sound check and not the actual show!

As soon as the music stopped my heart started beating so loudly that I was afraid the whole studio could hear it. But then I thought 'Now come on, Lorraine, you've always wanted to be on TV, so now you've got the chance, why be nervous and blow it?'

The music started to play again, only this time it was for real, and I recovered just in time, and found myself dancing as I'd never thought I could dance before! 9

Doris

6 When we arrived at the studio I was remarkably calm and collected. My only worry was my hair. How should I style it for such an important occasion?

We had half an hour to get ready before the show and I spent all of it playing about with different styles which the others didn't like, and which I didn't particularly like myself! Nothing worked, so at the very last moment I decided to wear it the same way as Deniece had hers. All that worry was for nothing! 9

Delroy

6 I remember getting up at 7.00 a.m., sorting through all my clothes and thinking, 'I haven't got a thing to wear!' I was at school at the time and all I ever wore were blue tank tops, white shirts and grey trousers, and I definitely wasn't going to wear any of those!

I told Dad, and of course he already had the problem in hand. He said we'd be able to go on a quick shopping spree as soon as we reached Birmingham. So some of the clothes I wore on that programme were genuine on-the-day buys from the Birmingham Bull Ring shopping centre. But don't ask me who picked them! 9

Stedman

6 At the end of the first number we did on *Pebble Mill* we went back to our dressing-rooms to change for our next song, 'Hide And Seek'. Imagine our surprise when, as we finished dressing, the show's producer popped in to tell us that during our performance lots of viewers had been ringing in to say how much they liked us!

Apparently they received a record number of phone calls about our performance that day – more than they had had about any band before! By the end of the evening we all felt pretty good, what with our performance and the great response we'd had. We were all looking forward to future TV shows we hoped would come along, and we realised that if you put your heart into something and do your best, everything really *does* turn out for the best. And that's the rule we've always gone by ever since. 9

TV Times At Pebble Mill

Did you ever see such a gloomy group at the end of their first TV show? Here we are in the Pebble Mill sitting-room having our last cup of delicious(!) BBC tea, and feeling more than a little sad that the show seemed to go so quickly. We'd performed 'Problematic' and 'Hide And Seek' as an unknown band – and emerged victorious in the eyes of the public!

This is better! Here we are on another *Pebble Mill* show later on in our career, dressed in more elaborate costumes, and raring to go! This particular performance was more like shooting a video because we had to dance our way around so many different locations all over the building. Quite frankly I'm surprised the producer didn't ask us to perform in the toilets!

Phew! Just one more location to go and we're off home. And guess where that last location is, fans? Why, it's up on the roof of course! Don't you sometimes wonder how we can work so hard and still manage to smile and keep our thumbs up at the end of the day? Well, to be honest, we're just relieved that the programme's over and they can't *ever* put us through such a gruelling routine again.

Back home there are still the household chores to be done! No wonder that when 5 Star lend a helping hand their parents run and hide. Well who wouldn't when you have a washing-up ordeal like this going on in your kitchen? You are probably thinking, 'Ah, at least we've discovered something that 5 Star *aren't* very good at!' but I'm sorry to disappoint you. The thing is, we all love doing the washing-up so much that we're actually fighting over who gets the dishcloth! This picture was taken in our old Romford home.

Welcome to Spaghetti Land

ON APRIL 16th, 1985, we flew from Heathrow Airport, London, to Italy, arriving at 7.00 p.m. in the pretty mountain resort of Riva del Garda, where we were to appear on Italian television for the first time.

We'd all been up and on the go since 5.30 a.m. so we were more than pleased to arrive in our warm hotel rooms, which had welcoming bunches of flowers, hot showers, and to top it all, balconies with the best view possible of Lake Garda.

But there wasn't much time for a rest. That same evening we had to make our way to rehearsals, and, having *no* idea how popular we were in Italy, we were totally unprepared for what was about to hit us.

Waiting outside the TV studio were hundreds of fans, pushing forward and shouting for autographs as we got off our bus. We got into the building safely enough, but trying to get out again was a different story! We waited ages for the fans to clear away but they persisted, getting ready to grab us, or anything belonging to us that they could lay their hands on!

All that lay between them and their trophies were a few wobbly metal barriers, and as soon as we dared to step outside, the fans rushed up to the barriers and screamed so loudly our ear-drums nearly burst! They were the most desperate fans I'd ever seen in all my years in show biz!

We had got half-way to our bus when the most devastating thing happened. The fans had pushed and shoved with such determination that the barriers came down!

Our bodyguards shouted at us to get back in the studio, but we decided to run for our lives! We made it into our bus in one piece (or rather, in five pieces!) and all agreed that it had been one of the most frightening experiences we'd encountered so far – and also one of the most exciting.

I remember thinking to myself – is this show business or *is* this show business?

This picture was taken outside the studio about two hours after the fans had finally cleared away!

Our view of the fans from the bus – just look at the determined expressions on their faces!

Five, four, three, two, one – and action! 5 Star go 'live on the air' on the *Riva del Garda* show, which went off perfectly. There's Stedman strutting his stuff and spotting a young, attractive Italian girl who (he hopes!) is giving him the eye.

Welcome to Spaghetti Land

We spent four whole days in Italy which turned out to be a lot of fun. This picture was taken at a photo session in the grounds of the Hotel du Lac. Just before it was taken, we'd all been busy trying to catch four stray kittens which were playing near by. Though we didn't succeed, we did manage to tempt them into playing with some twigs.

As you can tell, this bad photography doesn't quite fit in with the other excellent pieces displayed in this beautifully set out book (well I am a Gemini so you would expect just a *hint* of modesty!) and that's because it's not one of mine! It's Lorraine's, but don't tell anybody – it's a secret between you and me!

Welcome to Spaghetti Land

Here we are, resting our feet after a stroll around the town. Me, Lorraine and Doris had just been on a mad shopping spree for some genuine Italian handbags, but unfortunately, Lorraine and Doris both went and fell in love with the same white bag! So did this lead to a punch-up? (Nah, come one, they're grown girls!) They came to a compromise and bought the white bag and a red bag, but as you can see in the picture, Lorraine muscled in on the white bag. Sneaky!

I bet I know what you're thinking when you look at this picture – you're thinking, 'Look at 5 Star having such a wonderful time in all that Italian sunshine. Wish I was there!' Well, funnily enough, that's what I'm thinking too at the moment!

Here we are in the downstairs restaurant of our hotel, just after doing a TV recording in the shops; being mobbed by our fans on the street; and signing autographs near the river's edge!

Welcome to Spaghetti Land

Radio interviews: Us photographed with our favourite "Italiano" DJ. Ain't it!

Ah well, all good things have to come to an end and these were our 'time to go home' pics. As you can see, we were none of us very keen on the idea and there were miserable faces all round, especially Doris's! She actually covered her face as we boarded the airport bus so you wouldn't be able to see how upset she was. Still, as they say in Italian, 'Ciao!' (pronounced 'chow'), or as we said, 'Chow for now!'

We Love L.A.!

OUR FIRST album, *Luxury Of Life,* went platinum and so did our second, *Silk And Steel,* on October 7th 1986. We're the first band to have ever had nine consecutive hits within such a short period of time (just seventeen months) and this stands today as a new record in the music industry.

That second album was mostly recorded in America. On Saturday January 18th 1986, we flew to the wonderful sunny city of Los Angeles. We were escorted from the airport to our hotel in a luxurious white stretch Lincoln limousine, and as we stared out of the windows and tried to take everything in, we were totally in awe of the sights and the whole atmosphere of that amazing city.

We arrived at our hotel, Le Mondrian, just off Sunset Boulevard, at 7.00 p.m., and wasted no time ordering food from room service and exploring all the American TV channels on the set in our room.

But after the eight-hour flight our body clocks were telling us that it was the middle of the night, British time, and because we were so jet-lagged we soon found ourselves ready for some shut-eye. We had a busy day ahead of us, and I definitely needed my beauty sleep!

I was so confused by all the time changes that I woke up in the middle of the night, L.A. time, and suddenly felt wide awake. I woke Doris and asked her if it was time for me to go to the studio, and we wondered how come they had such dark afternoons in L.A.! We switched on the radio to try and find out the time and the D.J. was saying, 'Good morning, listeners,' but everything was so quiet, it didn't seem like morning, and when we looked out of the window, there was hardly any traffic outside.

I remember panicking and thinking to myself, 'Gosh, I'm going to be late, I'd better give Daddy a ring,' but then I made the mistake of lying down again and of course going straight back into a deep sleep.

Before I go any further, there is a strange little story I'd like to share with you. Something very mysterious occurred in that hotel room one night – are you ready for this, folks?

Doris and I were sharing a bedroom with Lorraine. We had one bed at one end of the room, and Lorraine had her own by the door. Late one night I suddenly

Dean Martin's star – one of the many commemorative paving stones on the famous Hollywood 'Walk Of Fame', and alongside it, the star of Vincent Price. Lorraine, being the Hollywood movie fanatic in the family, was particularly thrilled to be standing where so many of her favourite stars were remembered.

What have we here? It's Delroy, Doris, Lorraine and Stedman – four stars having a fab time walking on top of all the other stars' stars. But someone's missing. Where, you're probably wondering, is Deniece? Well it was a bit difficult for me to be in this picture since I was the one who took it. And it's a work of art, even if I say so myself!

felt a big bump on our bed and looked up to see Lorraine. I took one look at her face and thought I was having a nightmare (I'm being really cruel now!). Actually it was Lorraine who'd had the nightmare; she claimed she'd seen not one but *two* ghosts walking *through* the closed door, and she wanted to climb into bed with us because she was so frightened. She kept on and on nagging us but we wouldn't let her. How wicked of us, you may think, but we knew that if we gave in she'd nag us all night, because that's one thing our middle sister's very good at!

But back to business . . . we were in L.A. to record five songs: 'Are You Man Enough?', 'The Slightest Touch', 'Can't Wait', 'Find The Time' and 'Show Me'. On Sunday 19th, the day after we'd arrived, I went to the studio with Dad to sort out the vocals for each track, and that day and the next were spent putting the guide vocals down and recording the harmonies. Actually it got quite frustrating having to go in and out of the studio every day for four weeks, because naturally we were dying to do some sight-seeing!

During our second week in L.A. we received a personal visit from a songwriter called Michael Jay who'd brought a demo song for us called 'If I Say Yes', He'd originally written it with Whitney Houston in mind, but now he wanted us to do it instead.

We only had one day to learn it and two to record it, and as working all day in the studio really tires you and wears out your voice, we decided to finish it off in England. 'If I Say Yes' was recorded half in America and half in England, so it is different from all the rest.

We were in L.A. for a total of six weeks, during which we had to fit in lots of promotional work appearing in clubs and on radio and TV stations, as well as doing interviews for magazines and autograph-signing sessions in record shops. Phew! Fortunately there *was* just a little time left over for sightseeing. Here are some of the pictures we took during our stay.

We Love L.A.!

Deniece Pearson meets Bing Crosby, well, his hands and feet anyway! This was taken outside the famous Grauman's Chinese Theatre on Hollywood Boulevard. It was amazing for me too to be in the actual place where so many great actors and actresses have appeared. It made my visit to L.A. a really wonderful memory.

A picture of the late Steve McQueen's signature, and hand- and foot-prints, captured for an eternity in concrete!

Lorraine and Clark Gable. Her comments on the day? 'Being so close to all those famous people almost made me want to cry. I really feel I missed out on those golden days of Hollywood, I'd have given anything to have been born in those times. Ah well, perhaps in another life!'

Another one of Lorraine's faves, Mr Harold Lloyd. She says: 'I adored him in the old black and white movies because he was so funny, and those little round glasses gave him such a distinctive look.' She's just an old-fashioned girl! (But there's not much I can say about my photograph! One of my most 'rare' pieces and no doubt about it, I'll keep it that way!')

We Love L.A.!

Sitting around in hotel rooms gave these guys one helluva headache! (American speech is so infectious!) Well, what better cure than to take a quick stroll around the block to get our brains ready for action again. Here's a really neat little picture of us, just back from our jaunt with Mum. Hi, y'all!

Here we have 5 Star, or rather 2 Star, climbing aboard their ultra-flashy chauffeur-driven limo, fully equipped with a TV, drinks bar, swimming pool, tennis court... (nah, only joking!). Actually we were all on our way to the recording studio to work on our super-spectacular-fabadoo *Silk And Steel* album. Have a nice day!

Lorraine and Doris revive their vocal chords before a spot of recording. Belting out all those harmonies always leaves you a little hoarse!

This is the very microphone on which the whole of our *Silk And Steel* album was recorded. I'm going through the harmonies with Lorraine and Doris just before we go for an actual take.

We Love L.A.!

Here are Del and Sted – putting it all on again! They're quite deeply into rehearsing *this* morning because they'd skived off rehearsals the night before!

This is our producer, Richard Burgess, busily checking all the equipment before we launch into our next song. Well, we wouldn't want to waste our precious vocals on a faulty mike!

Now here's one of the people who wrote a track for the album. Her name's Sue Sheridan, and she wrote 'Show Me'. We met her while working at Laraby Studios, where we recorded six of our tracks.

Thumbs up to Michael Jay who wrote both 'The Slightest Touch' and 'If I Say Yes'. This man can write a mean tune or two!

We Love L.A.!

Here we have Dad accompanied by song writer Paul Gurvitz and a representative from Chrysalis Music, who came to meet us at the studio. Paul wrote 'Find The Time' and 'Are You Man Enough?'.

Another day, another music show! There we were *trying* to get a song recorded for our album, when suddenly we were dragged upstairs to do a TV interview! That's the presenter with us. It's a tough life being in a band, fans!

Down to business! Dad sorts out some studio dates when he can co-produce two of the album tracks with Michael Jay. That's Peter Robinson, sitting on the left, with whom we do a lot of work at BMC/RCA records.

This is *another* TV show we had to fit in whilst recording. As you can see, Sted looks completely worn out after having to wait an hour and a half for the TV crew to set up all their equipment. The rest of us are still in good spirits!

Two in the afternoon and it's feeding time back on the ranch! For all you nosey readers who'd like to know just exactly what we're eating – Lorraine's stuffing herself with a disgustingly healthy mixture of melon, oranges, mangoes, kiwi fruit, strawberries and vanilla ice-cream; Doris is munching into a fishburger with fries; and Delroy and I have got beefburgers with fries. Sick of her salad, Lorraine tries to move in on Del's burger but he swears he hasn't got any left. Until I discover that he's hiding it under the table! Here I am having a fit of hysteria and, umm, I think Delroy's just about to slap me round the face!

Having a Lovely

Now we move on to Detroit where we recorded the *Stars Of Tomorrow* show. (That's us, folks!)

While the cameramen weren't looking, Delroy, Doris and Stedman couldn't resist the chance to discover what it was like to work behind the scenes. Directing and producing are ambitions we'd all like to realise in the future.

This is the show's presenter, who said he was thrilled to bits to have us on his programme. Naturally!

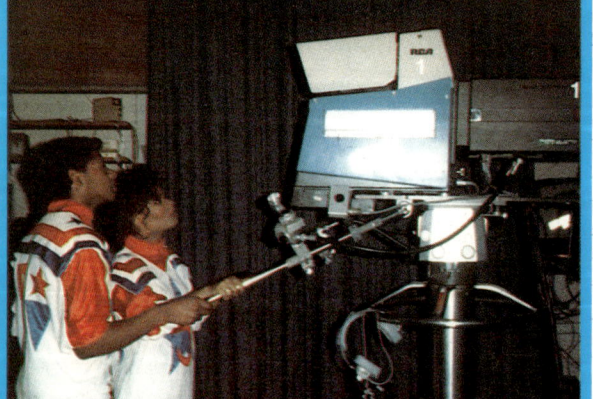

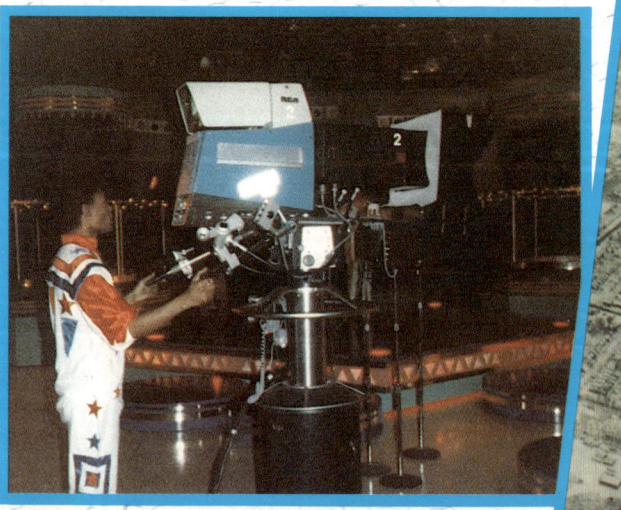

Time, in Detroit!

Finally the performance is over and here you see Doris and Mummy back at the hotel in the girls' room. They're looking through the room service menu to order some scrumptious food for everyone but, oh dear, looks as if Lorraine's spotted the Black Forest gateau. (She'd have that for breakfast if she had her way!)

This is the sign of a well-known pop radio station called 99 D.T.X., and it's the biggest in Detroit. We spent most of our last few weeks flying between L.A. and Detroit to broadcast on this, and many, many more stations. I get the feeling they liked us in Detroit!

Phew, fifty million autographs later! This was a P.A. (personal appearance) we did in a Detroit club; signing books, photos, records, you name it! Ever had writer's cramp?

This is a picture of Detroit taken just fifteen minutes before landing. It was odd flying from L.A., where the climate's hot and sunny, to dull old Detroit where it was freezing. One minute we'd be wearing T-shirts and eating ice-creams, and the next we'd be pulling on jumpers and scarves and having hot tea and biscuits! Can you imagine experiencing such drastic weather changes? But it was great when it came to pulling out all the summer clothes and shoving the winter ones back into the bottom of the suitcase!

Another day, another radio station! Here we had to sing a special radio commercial for our current single, 'Let Me Be the One'. Every little bit helps!

Having a Lovely Time in Detroit!

'Hey, man, aren't you Deniece from 5 Star?' Here are me and Lorraine with one of our number one fans at a club P.A. in Detroit.

Here we're posing with a journalist and the manager of a local Black Radio station. 'Let Me Be the One' had just entered the Top Twenty.

Is it *him* or isn't it? Well, unfortunately (for Doris!) it isn't. But this chappy does look remarkably like Michael Jackson, doesn't he? We met this lookalike while we were doing an in-store in Detroit. (News came back to us that he was actually following us to every gig we gave! Strange, eh?)

Altogether we went to fifteen different radio stations in Detroit. Here are shots from just a few of them. Once you've seen one radio station – you've seen them all!

Having a Lovely Time in Detroit!

Some of the Detroit 5 Star fanatics posing with us just outside their local record store, where we did yet another record-signing-poster-printing-autograph-hunting P.A.!

Are you ready for this? It's none other than the legendary *Soul Train* programme watched by soul fans throughout America, with five young people about to make their début.

Eleven in the morning and we're being picked up by the fab American limo in which we did most of our travelling while we stayed in the States. Soul Train – here we come!

As you can see, we've changed into our costumes ready for the show. But just before the programme we posed with some of the TV crew and our TV promoter Paula Batson from R.C.A. America.

The entire Pearson family pose with *Soul Train*'s famous presenter, Don Carnillias, just after our performance. *Soul Train* is so well-established it's as much a part of America as the Statue Of Liberty! Over the years it's captured performances by all the greats, from the Jackson Five to the stars of today! Now we too are part of their huge collection of stars on film.

Having a Lovely Time in Detroit!

Mummy and I look pretty pleased with ourselves here, don't we? We're sitting in the limo opposite Doris and Lorraine and wearing great big smiles of relief now that the show is over. Meanwhile, Doris is occupied watching the boys' car driving off back to the hotel.

Greetings from Florida!

Here we've just touched down in Miami, Florida. But sadly, Disney World's going to have to wait for a while because we've got so much work to do here! The three people in the middle are the promoters who'll be looking after us while we visit clubs and radio stations.

Here we're pictured with the owner of a club we appeared in in Florida. In this live performance we sang three tracks from our *Luxury of Life* album, and also met Jermaine Stewart who appeared in the club straight after us.

Okay, so it's only rehearsal time, but as usual, we're giving it our all! This is the stage we performed on that night, and afterwards, we met the famous producer known as Jelly Bean! Doris said: 'I thought he was going to be a great big tall man but, no, to my surprise, he was actually smaller than me!'

No, this isn't the Miami Vice Squad! This is our promotional team again, and this time we're outside another of the clubs we performed in.

We were each given a present for putting up with all the hard work and hassles we had to face in Miami! Tearing off the paper, what did we find inside? A Miami sweatshirt complete with a Miami Vice cap – how appropriate!

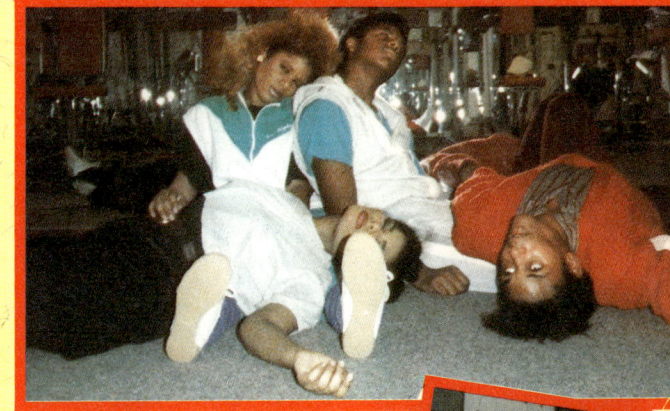

Macho Del poses. He never misses the lens! Here we are signing albums, posters, pictures and even hands and arms belonging to our eagerly awaiting Detroit fans in a local record store.

Well, wouldn't *you* be exhausted if you'd used all the apparatus in the hotel gym? There'll be a few stiff muscles tomorrow! Being a true Gemini – witty, clever, etc. – I'd played my cards right and stuck to the bike!

At the end of our hectic work schedule, Daddy got together with R.C.A's A.&R. man Peter Robinson to chat about our achievements in America so far. They say actions speak louder than words, and from the smug looks on these two faces, I'd say we hadn't done too badly. As Daddy said to Peter: 'I think you'll have to agree there's *no* stopping 5 Star!'

Greetings from Florida!

As the sun rose on the morning of our departure, we felt it was shining specially for us as a fond farewell. We all woke early that morning to get ready to leave Los Angeles. Our destination was home sweet home, and in the lower picture you can see us arriving back in England.
(P.S. My picture of the sun is one of the photos of which I'm proudest. I've included it here because the scene was much too beautiful to keep to myself.)

Bonjour from Montreux

There were soon to be more adventures in store for us. It wasn't long before we were invited to perform at the famous Montreux pop festival, and this is the logo of the luxurious hotel we stayed in for three days, the Montreux Palace. (The photo shows the carpet ouside the hotel room!)

Here we are arriving in Switzerland, and from our dazed expressions, I'd say we were suffering from jet lag. Perhaps we hadn't really recovered from America!

Our first day in Montreux and already it's time for a photo session. We were actually knee-deep in photographers but enjoying every moment! Because of all the attention we received we felt like E.I.P.s – that's Extra Important People!

Bonjour from Montreux

On our second day we did more photo sessions, both indoors and out. On one of our trips outside we suddenly found ourselves trapped against a tree by an unexpected camera crew. Excuse us, fellas, but we've got a show to do!

Returning from a hard day's posing, we spotted this jewellery shop and couldn't resist gazing at the exceedingly smart Swiss watches and beautiful rings on display. (We couldn't resist spending, either!)

Bonjour from Montreux

View from a bridge! Here we're taking a well-deserved short break from one of the TV shows we appeared on.

5 Star join Mike Smith in the foyer of the Hyatt Hotel, the very place where A-ha were staying at the time! We were there to do an interview for Radio 1 (and I was there to keep an eye out for Morten!)

Bonjour from Montreux

From the sublime to the ridiculous. Can you imagine waking up in the morning to the peace and tranquillity of the Swiss mountains – and then having to drive back to the airport amidst the ghastly noise and fumes of early morning traffic? Talk about culture shock!

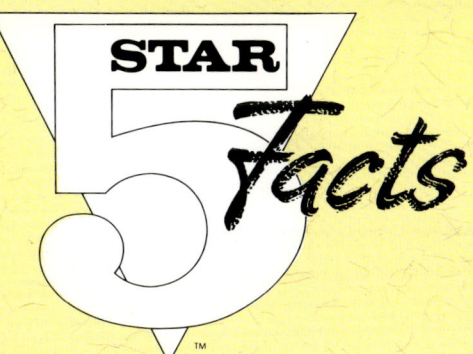

5 STAR Facts

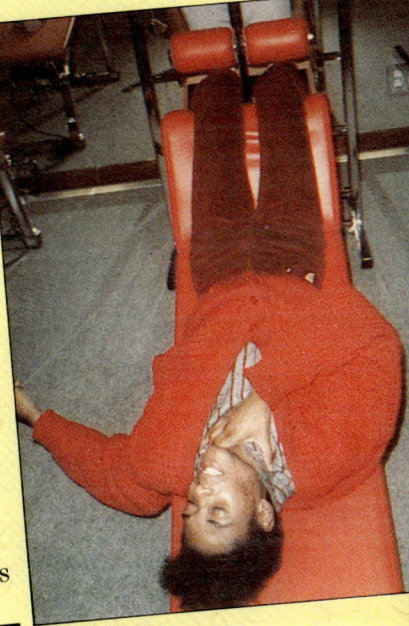

NAME: Stedman Pearson Jnr.

SPECIAL JOB IN 5 STAR: Main costume designer.

BIRTH DATE: June 29th 1964.

COLOUR OF HAIR: Black.

COLOUR OF EYES: Dark brown.

FAVOURITE HOBBY: Collecting cars.

FAVOURITE SPORT: Athletics, especially the 100 metres and 4 × 100 metres relay.

FAVOURITE FILM: *Oxford Blues.*

FAVOURITE FLOWER: Red rose.

FAVOURITE COLOUR: Cream.

FAVOURITE ITEM OF CLOTHING: Jumper.

DO YOU HAVE A GIRLFRIEND? No.

WHAT IS YOUR IDEAL GIRL LIKE? Like my mother.

WHAT KIND OF CAR DO YOU HAVE? An Audi Quattro.

DO YOU PLAY ANY INSTRUMENTS? Sometimes play keyboards.

HAVE YOU WON ANY CERTIFICATES OR MEDALS? Yes, for athletics and dancing.

WHERE DO YOU LIKE TO GO FOR AN EVENING OUT? To a hotel for dinner, and, when abroad, for a walk at night on the beach.

WHAT WAS YOUR WORST EXPERIENCE? Having my jacket torn by screaming fans.

WHAT IS YOUR AMBITION? To become successful in whatever I do, whether it is performing or business.

NAME: Doris May Pearson.

SPECIAL JOB IN 5 STAR: Choreographer.

BIRTH DATE: June 8th 1966.

COLOUR OF HAIR: Black.

COLOUR OF EYES: Dark brown.

FAVOURITE HOBBY: Rock climbing.

FAVOURITE SPORT: Basketball.

FAVOURITE FILM: *Moses.*

FAVOURITE FLOWER: Yellow rose.

FAVOURITE COLOUR: Green.

FAVOURITE ITEM OF CLOTHING: Jumper or jacket – to keep me warm!

DO YOU DO YOUR OWN MAKE-UP? Yes.

DO YOU HAVE A BOYFRIEND? No.

WHAT IS YOUR IDEAL MAN LIKE? Intelligent.

WHAT KIND OF CAR DO YOU HAVE? A Merc.

DO YOU PLAY ANY INSTRUMENTS? No.

HAVE YOU WON ANY CERTIFICATES OR MEDALS? Yes, medals for winning netball rallies, rounders teams and basket ball and a certificate for relay.

WHERE DO YOU LIKE TO GO FOR AN EVENING OUT? For a walk.

WHAT WAS YOUR WORST EXPERIENCE? Haven't had any.

WHAT IS YOUR AMBITION? To be more ambitious!

NAME: Lorraine Samantha Jean Pearson.
SPECIAL JOB IN 5 STAR: Songwriter.
BIRTH DATE: August 10th 1967.
COLOUR OF HAIR: Black.
COLOUR OF EYES: Dark Brown.
FAVOURITE HOBBY: Writing books and songs, and watching films.
FAVOURITE SPORT: High jump.
FAVOURITE FILM: *The Philadelphia Story*.
FAVOURITE FLOWER: Rose.
FAVOURITE COLOUR: Blue.
FAVOURITE ITEM OF CLOTHING: Jumpers – I look great in them!
DO YOU DO YOUR OWN MAKE-UP? Yes.
DO YOU HAVE A BOYFRIEND? No.
WHAT IS YOUR IDEAL MAN LIKE? He has two legs, a nice face and three arms!
WHAT KIND OF CAR DO YOU HAVE? A Ferrari.
DO YOU PLAY ANY INSTRUMENTS? No.
HAVE YOU WON ANY CERTIFICATES OR MEDALS? Yes, medals for winning netball rallies, rounders teams and basket ball and a certificate for high jump.
WHERE DO YOU LIKE TO GO FOR AN EVENING OUT? For a walk in the park.
WHAT WAS YOUR WORST EXPERIENCE? Getting fat!
WHAT IS YOUR AMBITION? To be part of the greatest pop group ever!

NAME: Deniece Lisa Maria Pearson.
SPECIAL JOB IN 5 STAR: Vocal arranger.
BIRTH DATE: June 13th 1968.
COLOUR OF HAIR: Black.
COLOUR OF EYES: Dark brown.
FAVOURITE HOBBY: Song-writing, playing instruments and writing books.
FAVOURITE SPORT: Tennis and roller skating.
FAVOURITE FILM: *E.T.* and *The Wizard of Oz*.
FAVOURITE FLOWER: Blue rose.
FAVOURITE COLOUR: Red.
FAVOURITE ITEM OF CLOTHING: Dresses. I like Marilyn Monroe and would like to look like her!
DO YOU DO YOUR OWN MAKE-UP? Yes, always for TV and videos.
DO YOU HAVE A BOYFRIEND? No. But I will have quite soon.
WHAT IS YOUR IDEAL MAN LIKE? Tall, of medium build, loving, caring and very special.
WHAT KIND OF CAR DO YOU HAVE? I don't have a car yet.
DO YOU PLAY ANY INSTRUMENTS? Yes, keyboards and guitar.
HAVE YOU WON ANY CERTIFICATES OR MEDALS? Yes, medals for netball, rounders and basket ball and a certificate for hurdles.
WHERE DO YOU LIKE TO GO FOR AN EVENING OUT? To a quiet and little-known restaurant.
WHAT WAS YOUR WORST EXPERIENCE? Being pulled off stage in concert.
WHAT IS YOUR AMBITION? To become a very well-known film producer, actress, song producer, songwriter, and win loads of Grammy and B.P.I. awards.

NAME: Delroy Pearson.
SPECIAL JOB IN 5 STAR: Producer and engineer.
BIRTH DATE: April 11th 1970.
COLOUR OF HAIR: Black.
COLOUR OF EYES: Dark brown.
FAVOURITE HOBBY: Fishing.
FAVOURITE SPORT: Football.
FAVOURITE FILM: Action films.
FAVOURITE FLOWER: Rose.
FAVOURITE COLOUR: Blue.
FAVOURITE ITEM OF CLOTHING: Jumper.
DO YOU HAVE A GIRLFRIEND? No.
WHAT IS YOUR IDEAL GIRL LIKE? Intelligent and pretty.
WHAT KIND OF CAR DO YOU HAVE? A Mercedes Cosworth.
DO YOU PLAY ANY INSTRUMENTS? Yes, keyboards, drums and guitar.
HAVE YOU WON ANY CERTIFICATES OR MEDALS? Yes, for football.
WHERE DO YOU LIKE TO GO FOR AN EVENING OUT? To London, for a meal.
WHAT WAS YOUR WORST EXPERIENCE? A car accident.
WHAT IS YOUR AMBITION? I don't know yet!